HUMAN STRIKE HAS ALREADY BEGUN & OTHER WRITINGS

CLAIRE FONTAINE

GW00750538

A collaboration between Mute & the Post-Media Lab

Mute

Please email mute@metamute.org with any details of
republication

Co-published as a collaboration between Mute and the
Post-Media Lab, Leuphana University.
PML Books is a book series to accompany the work of the
Post-Media Lab. http://postmedialab.org

Print ISBN: 978-1-906496-88-3
Also available as eBook ISBN: 978-1-906496-89-0

Distribution Please contact mute@metamute.org for trade and
distribution enquiries

Acknowledgements

Series Editors Clemens Apprich, Josephine Berry Slater,
Anthony Iles and Oliver Lerone Schultz
Layout Raquel Pérez de Eulate
Design Template Based on a template by Atwork
Cover Image Claire Fontaine, *Redemptions* (Horde), 2013
Photo credit Johnna Arnold

PML Books

The PML Book series is a collaboration between Mute
magazine and Post-Media Lab. The Lab was set up in
September 2011 and explores how post-broadcast media can
be used to intensify 'collective assemblages of enunciation'
– an idea originally formulated by Félix Guattari, and now
unfolding in diverse ways across the ubiquity of media.

During the course of the Lab's activity we will be publishing
two large anthologies, the first comprising a reader on the
concept of 'post-media', and the second summarising and
documenting the activity of the Lab.

The *Post-Media Anthology* collects writings by Adilkno,
Clemens Apprich, Alejo Duque, Felipe Fonseca, Gary Genosko,
Michael Goddard, Félix Guattari, Brian Holmes, Cadence
Kinsey, Oliver Lerone Schultz, Howard Slater, Rasa Smite and
Raitis Smits. (Forthcoming, ISBN 978-1-906496-94-4)

Alongside these larger publications we will be publishing a
series of four short titles by single authors addressing specific
themes:

- Digital Networks: Connecting People Apart
- The Subsumption of Sociality
- The Question of Organisation After Networks
- Life vs. Object: Comrade Things and Alien Life

The first books in this short series are:

Felix Stalder, *Digital Solidarity*,
(Forthcoming, ISBN 978-1-906496-92-0)

Claire Fontaine, *Human Strike Has Already Begun & Other
Writings*, (ISBN 978-1-906496-88-3)

The PML Book series is just one of several outlets for the
Lab's exploration of post-media strategies and conditions,
which includes fellowships, a virtual lab structure,
multiple collaborations, events, group readings and other
documentation.

For more information see: www.postmedialab.org/publications

MUTE BOOKS   PML Books

The Post-Media Lab is part of the Lüneburg Innovation
Incubator, a major EU project within Leuphana University of
Lüneburg, financed by the European Regional Development
Fund and co-funded by the German federal state of
Lower Saxony.

CONTENTS

FOREWORD

What follows is a selection of texts with different stories and different intentions. They are all sediments in the margin of something else, which remains liquid or gaseous, probably more important than the rest.

The practice of writing can only pursue the processes of thought and it rarely catches their tails. Human strike is not even a possible prey for it, since in any case it remains a horizon, a possibility, a disquieting guest, that cannot (and doesn't need to) be described by the written word. The traces left by this phenomenon find their own scriveners: human strike is not the invention of an author, it's actually what proves that any form of hypostasised individuality is nothing but a dirty compromise, the result of indecent commerce with some power. What truly counts in the economy of freedom are human relationships, what happens *between* people.

Radical theory is composed of texts that wish to accompany experimental practices - preserving the space of their potentiality, trying not to prevent things from happening by predicting them - and other texts that prescribe and show the way, texts that exterminate mistakes and kill questions.

The writings that are grouped here don't belong to any of these categories, maybe because they aren't 'radical' and they are not exactly theory. What they try to do is capture the space in which subjectivity opposes power and by doing so transforms itself into something other that doesn't even need to fight the same enemy, because this enemy cannot damage it nor access it. These moments can be rare and volatile, they don't accumulate, they don't become a system, but what is certain is that this exercise can highlight what will save us.

Today if subjectivity doesn't become simultaneously the weapon and the battlefield, the means and the end of every struggle, we will remain the embarrassed hostages to hope in social and political movements, with their tragic incapability to build a present that isn't just another state of exception. Militancy has shown that even within the most sincere and passionate quest for freedom relationships remain instrumental and therefore deadly. And even if the end is liberation, its tragic separation from the means transforms it into the worst slavery. Patriarchy has put everything to work: feelings, bodies, friendship, love, motherhood. And everything – within that libidinal economy – is nothing but a work of reproduction and preservation of the world as it is. The task of human strike is to defunctionalise all these useful activities and return them to their quintessential creativity that will unhinge any form of oppression.

Human strike is not a strategy and it's not a tactic, it has always already begun when we join it because it has always been there. Politicising its protean forms is the task that we can assume: recognising it in our spontaneous and unconscious behaviours, letting ourselves be nourished by the energy that every pertinent refusal emits.

The absurdity of the crisis we are living in is nothing but the confirmation of the necessity to coordinate these gestures. Police brutality and governments' ruthlessness can seem surprising when they shamefully present themselves as the only answer to a disaster entirely created by the ones in power.

In fact there is no possibility of having a dialogue with an organised power that, for the first time in many decades, explicitly betrays all over the planet even the most superficial illusion of democracy and honesty. A dialogue with the very iron fist that strangles the masses and progressively wipes out the conquests of workers' struggles is totally impossible. What is needed is a change of nature of the subjectivities where this power plants its seeds and plunges its roots.

If fascism could be eradicated it is because the subjectivities that embodied it at a certain point refused to reproduce it, broke with their past, decided that a new dream of cohabitation, another idea of mankind had to be born. If fascism hasn't been totally defeated it is because patriarchy and the colonisation of life by commodity are still our daily bread.

The possibilities that a concerted human strike could uncover are virtually unlimited. We cannot know what could happen if we did agree to change ourselves and change each other, because the very categories at our disposal today aren't the ones we will use in this possible future. Human strike will change the way we have to apprehend it, it will be a psychosomatic transformation, extremely difficult to criminalise and extremely contaminating. It will not happen through mysticism, through alternative techniques of the self, through a specific training, through the reappropriation of violence, but it might also happen because of these practices, although it will not be their direct result. What is at stake is the discovery of a new intimacy with ourselves that will make us resistant to cruelty and retaliation as much as lucid in front of abuses, flexible and detached, freed from the need to follow instructions or leaders. The experience of unlearning, which is necessary to spark this change, will require the abandonment of all superstitions, including the belief in revolution or the possibility of communism as it has been dreamt of through the past couple of centuries.

The refusal to reproduce models of the past, to represent a position or a group, will bring a new abstraction, a new imageless practice on the scene of politics, which will connect us to the consciousness that human strike is already happening, that it happens all the time, that we just need to listen to it and play it, like one plays in an orchestra or on a stage, as we all have a place in it. And the human strike needs us as much as we need it.

San Francisco, November 2012

THIS IS NOT THE BLACK BLOC

I. Semblances

4 February 2007, on the 8 o'clock news I see what appears to be a male figure, filmed from above, throwing stones in a night lit by flames. He is wearing a very elegant Dolce & Gabbana bomber-jacket with a big silver D&G on the back and an immaculate white ski-mask. This figure takes off to join another character who is wearing a black scarf over his face, a very beautiful orange knit hat, rather snug red-and-black plaid pleated trousers, and a chic navy-blue blazer, if I recall correctly. Soon after I see people charging an ambulance and an orange spot catches my eye again, but this time it's the colour of the nurses' uniforms trying to stop these people who are determined to remove the wounded in order to finish them off.

Fragments of images from Italy, from Catania, of the end of a soccer match where someone killed a carabiniere. Al Jazeera, it was announced, reported this news. Someone killed a carabiniere during the riots and that someone is from a strange hotbed, he is a supporter of the far-right wing, Nazi, fascist, revolutionary. On the same day in Baghdad, something much worse but less rare took place. The nightly news is over.

I open a newspaper, it's an old tabloid from January, the photos are superb, in particular those of a fellow called Scary Guy whom schools pay $1000 a day to come and preach peace in England, the USA, Australia... Scary Guy is a tattoo artist who was rejected by tattoo circles for having tattooed his face – an inexplicable taboo for that community. This rejection made him violent, hateful, up until the (fuzzy) moment when he prepared his conversion and decided to speak about peace. I can't tell if he is a real policeman or not, but the photos show him wearing a blue T-shirt with the word 'Police' embroidered in white on the chest; he also has piercings on his eyebrows and the bridge of his nose.

Is Scary Guy a clown – in the same way that Arendt referred to Eichmann? Is he a punk dressed like a cop who is going to discourage schoolboys from bullying?

In *The Coming Community*, Agamben describes Limbo as it is depicted in Saint Thomas. The souls that inhabit this region of the Beyond are not stricken with afflictions because they have done no wrong. However, they are deprived of the greatest good, which is the contemplation of God – yet they are unaware of their plight so they do not suffer from it. They suffer no more than a normal man grieves over not being able to fly.

While my eyes follow the footsteps of customers going to the Black Bloc boutique at the entrance to the Palais de Tokyo, on the brushed concrete, under the high ceiling, Agamben's words about the souls in Limbo automatically pop into my head: 'like letters without addressees...they remained without destiny.'

II. Impressions

Scary Guy tells the children he indoctrinates about social peace for $1000 a day: you shouldn't trust appearances, but you *really* shouldn't trust them. You see me like this, piercing-tattoos, dreadful-looking, yeah, well you've got it wrong, I am Gandhi and the Pope rolled up into one, I've come to deliver the good word, and you will love each other, and you will forget all about your crushed, frustrated childhoods, abandoned to the solitude of TV and video games, you will repress yourselves even more so you can start turning into good little robots right away.

Well, he doesn't say that, but the children understand that.

He is like a big brother, the terrifying chap, the big brother that we should have had, we the unhappy ones. We should have met him when we were ten years old so we could get that tattoos and piercings are not rebellious gestures, that police is a mode of being for everyone rather than a profession, that what counts is not just finding one's place in society as it stands, without criticising it (changing it, even less so), what counts is inventing one's own place in it, if nobody offers you one. It doesn't even matter if it's a paradoxical and insulting place, as long as it's not in opposition, doesn't contest anything.

Because, after all, life has no meaning, it is like a facial tattoo, like the money we have or don't have, life is arbitrary and hopeless, and that's why one mustn't rebel, what's the point?

And so, getting back to the strange shop in the 16th arrondissement in Paris that has this name, Black Bloc, which I just don't get – surely its owners must have thought they had to do some sort of special thing to make museum visitors understand that they shouldn't trust appearances either. For example: giving a place like that a name that evokes transgression or even the destruction of merchandise, while here we are selling our merchandise at high prices and we're loving it. Or maybe the black bloc sounded a bit like the opposite of the white cube, or the idea of a black bloc is suggestive, martial, what do I know? And that the two words in English have a lovely musical ring to them, or something.

It's not just appearances one shouldn't trust, one shouldn't trust words either. Or more specifically, the link we imagine exists between words and images, between the visible and the sayable. For example, even if we believe we've found the illustration of this concept in photographs of marching people dressed in black, black bloc is a word without an image. The term black bloc alludes to a manifestation of desire for collective opacity, a will not to appear and to materialise affects that are increasingly hard to take. The black bloc is not a visual object, it's an object of desire.

III. Translations

It's not that these two words are stripped of meaning, they have meaning – 'black bloc' means a black bloc – but as soon as they are written down or spoken they show they have been orphaned from their context and that we can do whatever we please with them. Surely because we are dealing with a translation from German. On the other hand, *schwarze Block* means something, it roots us in a history of resistance bound up with the two 20th century Germanies. For while meaning is not lacking from translations, *autonomy* often is. In the movement from one language to another, sometimes meaning is deported despite itself gets injured, and occasionally dies. The violence of the act of translating allies itself on a point with the violence of commercial transactions: one presupposes there is an *equivalence* between words from different languages, but one winds up colliding with the incommensurable in singular histories.

I could tell you that *schwarze Block* was a tactical form, that it was a means of preventing the police from identifying and isolating who committed what gesture during a riot. I could tell you that dressing in black meant: we are all comrades, we are all in solidarity, we are all alike, and this equality liberates us from the responsibility of accepting a fault we do not deserve; the fault of being poor in a capitalist country, the fault of being anti-fascist in the fatherland of Nazism, the fault of being libertarian in a repressive country. That it meant: nobody deserves to be punished for these reasons, and since you are attacking us we are forced to protect ourselves from violence when we march in the streets. Because war, capitalism, labour regulations, prisons, psychiatric hospitals, those things are not violent, however you see those of us who want to freely live our homosexuality, the refusal to found a family, collective life and the abolition of property as the violent ones.

So, if you want to arrest me instead of my comrade just because we are wearing the same clothing, go ahead, I accept that, I don't deserve to be punished because he doesn't deserve it either... I could go on like this, and even provide you with more specifics, by supplementing it with the history of demonstrations, of victories, with dates to back it all up and everything, like the time a band was playing around the rioters in the deserted streets, or the time when the police took off running... I could go on for pages and pages, but that's not the issue here. All this isn't the black bloc.

Instead, let's ask what 'this is the black bloc' means? Who says that? Wouldn't that be a definition like an image filmed from a window, like the one from the 8 o'clock news on 4 February 2007 and so many others, a definition shot from above, taken from the viewpoint of a watchtower, from some panopticon? What we are describing is always a block of ant-men, cockroach-men, a black block, which is black like the earth because it is seen from afar. But the carabinieri, they are also a black bloc. Baudelaire said that his contemporaries dressed in dark clothes that no painter enjoyed depicting, were an army of undertakers, that they were all celebrating some funeral. Enamoured undertakers, revolutionary undertakers.

IV. Silences

No speech comes 'from inside' the black bloc because there is no inside or outside. The black bloc, which we name as such with these two impoverished words, is not constituted like groups, corps, institutions. It is a temporary agglomeration without truth or watchwords. It is also what is left in the hands of our discontent, at the stage of society we have reached, despite ourselves:

the impossibility of marching together while shouting out phrases so that they can be heard, the incapacity of engaging in indirect and representative actions, the urgent need to unload one-thousandth of the cruelty the State, money, and advertising inject in all our veins every day.

The category black bloc doesn't designate anything or anyone, or more precisely, maybe it designates *anyone as such.* A distinctive feature of one who finds themselves in what we call a black bloc is to demand nothing for themselves or for others, to cut across public space without being subjected to it for once, to disappear in a mass that has at last come together in places that are not office or factory exits and public transportation at rush hour. Rampant hypocrisy makes us associate the black bloc with a specific and organised entity – like Sony, Vivendi, or Total Fina – and this same hypocrisy considers as 'crimes' the minor damage that the desire for wilful indistinctness leaves behind when it takes the form of a spontaneous demonstration.

In this night where all demonstrators look alike there is no point in posing Manichean questions. Especially since we know that the distinction between guilty and innocent no longer matters, all that counts is the one between winners and losers. Punishment always lands on the latter, not because they deserve it but because somebody has to be repressed. Trying to figure out if someone has infiltrated a black bloc is like trying to know the extent to which rain infiltrates a river, a lake or seawater.

V. Repetitions

Some days I flip through certain art magazines: glossy paper, squeaky clean, repetitions and very few differences, but it doesn't matter. These papers are made to put one in the mood, like certain soft drugs. And in the mood, one discovers a particular kind of omnivorous, but levelling, visual sophistication. All things become equally appreciable once delicately placed on the white rectangle of their pages, the forms and colours travel from the white cube to this new square and they have everything to gain there.

One mustn't believe that the vision of the world of these papers excludes radicality, even in its explicitly political form. But this radicality is only a shadow of 'what one should detect of it', and never an expression of what it is possible to do with it. It is inevitably a question of taking distance from this radicality, not because it's needed to show that we do not go along with it, but because the problem isn't even one of hearing its message, one must simply judge *its tone*. And the tone is always monotonous or excited.

Why are you shouting, damn it, if we know that things are the way they are? We already know: stop yelling! Disappear or turn into your image, so we can turn down the sound or put some music on instead, if necessary.

These papers don't have their own voices, but that's how they would speak if they started to speak, and it is not even because of cynicism, but because of lack of experience. The authors of articles, who consider themselves clever theoreticians, anti-conformist or disabused intellectuals, ignore the ways words affect bodies to the point of generating the ordinary miracle of mobilisation and the extraordinary one of insurrection. These articles are a form of disguised pornography, in so far as whenever we are dealing with the least communicable moments, when everyone is bare and everyone is the same, and all the bodies are indistinctly breathing together, we can say whatever we want about it because we *always already* know what we want to see there. It's this violence that is as obscene, superficial and brutal as an identity check.

And this is how the most depleted sophistication, which says it's above the need for making claims, traces the heartless and odourless broad geopolitical picture and ends up finding all direct action folkloric and detestable. This viewpoint considers from the wearied aesthete position the rage-filled gesticulations of those who have no other choice but to scream, smash things and move in packs on the streets.

The hermeneutics of the complex archipelagos of dissension is knowledge that has already disappeared: we no longer need to investigate the reasons, the genealogies, the aspirations of those who revolt outside of associations and unions, it is much easier to criminalise them in the name of democracy and everyone's solitude. Therefore, the formerly respectable 'critical' tradition, meant to sharpen the weapons of the mind and ally them to the masses through avant-garde action when the time is right, has been submerged by forgetting. Putting insurrections into words has simply turned into a not very attractive task. For one revolts first and foremost because words are insufficient.

No desubjectivisation can bridge the abyss that has grown between the critique of social movements and their reality. Once we judge the unique and exceptional moments of autonomous movements with the measure we use for ordinary life moments, we are in the process of constructing the logical and political circle that closes in on its own idiocy. No translation is capable of converting actions into words, for their separation is the daily tragedy of our democratic regimes. In order to approach the uncertain territory of rebellion, we must first honour the disjunction between everyone's words, images and gestures. For the geography of these gaps houses the prospect of knowledge that transforms those who hold it and renders them capable of liberty.

The black bloc is you, when you stop believing in it.

Paris, 1 April 2007

HUMAN STRIKE HAS ALREADY BEGUN

'Grève humaine' is the French expression for 'human strike', designating the most generic movement of revolt against any oppressive condition. It's a more radical and less specific strike than a general strike or a wildcat strike.

Human strike attacks the economic, affective, sexual and emotional positions within which subjects are imprisoned. It provides an answer to the question 'how do we become something other than what we are?' It isn't a social movement although within the uprising and agitations it can find a fertile ground upon which to develop and grow, sometimes even against these.

For example, it has been said that the feminist movement in Italy during the 1970s demolished the leftist political organisations, but what hasn't been said is what leftist political organisations were doing to the women who were part of them. Human strike can be a revolt within a revolt, an unarticulated refusal, an excess of work or the total refusal of any labour, depending on the situation. There is no orthodoxy for it. If strikes are made in order to improve specific aspects of the workers' conditions, they are always a means to an end. But human strike is a pure means, a way to create an immediate present here where there is nothing but waiting, projecting, expecting, hoping.

Adopting a behaviour that doesn't correspond to what others tell us about ourselves is the first step of the human strike: the libidinal economy, the secret texture of values, lifestyles and desires hidden by the political economy are the real plane of consistency of this revolt.

'We need to change ourselves': everyone agrees on this point, but who to become and what to produce are the first questions that arise as soon as this discussion takes place in a collective context. The reflex of refusing any present that doesn't come with the guarantee of a reassuring future is the very mechanism of the slavery we are caught in and that we must break. To produce the present is not to produce the future.

'How do I do it and where do I start?' Surely everyone knows this better for oneself than anybody else ever could: no more leaders, no more teachers, no more students, here comes the time of inventing new mediations between people, and we are already in the midst of the work of the human strike. There are no preliminaries, no intermediary steps, no organisers in charge of the logistical aspects. The work of the human strike strikes against itself. It transforms at the same time what we see and the organs we see with. It transforms both ourselves and the people who made this transformation possible. It kills the bourgeois in all of us, liberating unknown forces.

Explaining what human strike is, how to map it, how to articulate it, is like giving a technical lesson of sexual education to the person we wish to seduce. It is like describing to ourselves the overwhelming ocean of our possible madness whilst sitting safely on the shore. A female voice from the movement of '77 said:

> The return of the repressed threatens all my projects of work, research, politics. Does it threaten them or is it the truly political thing in myself, to which I should give relief and

room? [...] Silence brought the failure of this part of myself that desired to make politics, but it affirmed something new. There has been a change, I have started to speak out, but during these days of silence I felt that the affirmative part of myself was occupying the entire space again. I convinced myself of the fact that the mute woman is the most fertile objection to our politics. The non-political digs tunnels that we mustn't fill with earth.

Writing about the human strike is itself the experience of a double bind, it's like walking on a suspended wire between making things possible and exorcising them through language.

There are no lessons of human strike, it is nothing but a disquieting possibility that we must remain intimate with. We are remunerated neither for the work of love nor for being able to find the right words to bridge the social fractures that separate all of us. We do not get paid for making everyday life more enjoyable or simply possible for ourselves and for other people. The unremunerated labour of the affects continuously crushes the insulting pyramid of capitalistic values but this conflict is effaced day after day.

Without the mothers' excess of love for their children there would be no one left to exploit. Without the refusal to believe that we can still communicate non-commercial sensations and feelings to each other, the prostitutional business of advertising would lack even the syntax to make itself understandable. Wherever it takes place, human strike declares the end of the criminal fiction of the equivalence between money and time, money and space, money and food, money and bodies.

If the current negotiations on the right to pollute the planet have just reached a dead end, we could already read in a French newspaper on 11 May 2009 that:

> in order not to ignore the irreparable damage that the development of industrial civilization causes to the ecosystem, we have decided to put a price on the natural resources that are pillaged day by day. It's established that one hectare of forest is worth 970 euros and that one hectare of meadow is worth 600 euros. It's established that the value of the extinction of the bees is calculated on the basis of the cost of artificial pollination made by humans.

There was no mention of the cost of the extinction of the humans who would not know what a bee is, its presence in the warm air, its colours, the wax, the honey, the flowers inclining under its weight or the meaning of Mandeville's tale. No logical movement can oppose such a state of things, a new wave of irrational actions must disorganise the ordinary progression of the disaster. Human strike simply declares the effective bankruptcy of the market economy that pretends to own life but endlessly annihilates it.

No mourning of the impossible revolutions can get in the way of the human strikers because human strike is not a mission, nor a project or a program. It is the gesture that makes legible the silent political element in everything: women's lives, the dissatisfaction of rich people, the anger of privileged teenagers, the refusal to submit to the mediocrity of necessity, ordinary racism, and so on.

When we inhabit language we place ourselves on the permeable membrane between life and desires, where it clearly appears that life and desires are made of the same fabric. Desiring together makes things come true even when they are not technically true. Witches were burned for having truly been flying in the night and for having actually kissed Satan's ass. When we come out of prison we are delinquents, even if we were innocents when they first arrested us by mistake.

We constantly become what other people want us to be, but starting a human strike means inverting that movement and refusing to act upon the actions of others through the use of power; it means opposing a philosophy of management with the material presence of potentiality. Reality can be more than what any realistic representation of the facts offers. The very concept of reality progressively starts to fade when we loose touch with the possible and the impossible that human strike points to.

NYC, 17 December 2009

HUMAN STRIKE WITHIN THE FIELD OF THE LIBIDINAL ECONOMY

The possibility of keeping together autonomy and an affective life is a tale that hasn't been written yet.
– Lea Melandri, Una visceralità indicibile, 2007

In 1974 François Lyotard published the surprising book entitled *Libidinal Economy* where he attacked Marxist and Freudian simplifications and he opened a new perspective on the connection between desires and struggle. What starts to crumble at that time under the offensive of the two essential weapon-books by Deleuze and Guattari *Anti-Oedipus* and *A Thousand Plateaus* is the fetishisation of consciousness as the organ that will lead the revolution. As the myth of the avant-garde begins to decline, a psychosomatic reorganisation arises and its consequences on the relationship between people are brutal and inevitable. Like in an inverted Menenius Agrippa's speech, the head, with all its metaphorical connotations, lost its privilege and the low body could find a new voice full of desire and fear. A new materialism was coming to life inside people's bodies. At this point the failure of the responsible and pyramidal militant structures becomes blatant: thirst for power, need for leaders and the insufficiency of language to resolve conflicts inside the groups reveal the impossibility of living and fighting in such formations. In '73 the Gramsci Group called for a different way of doing politics:

it's no longer possible to talk to each other from avant-garde to avant-garde with a sectary language of 'expert' politicians [...] and then not be able to talk concretely about our experiences. The consciousness and the explanation of things must become clear through the experience of one's own condition, one's own problems and needs, not only through theories that describe mechanisms.[1]

The language that served the purposes of traditional politics seemed to have lost all its use value in the mouths of these young people; the members of the militant groups felt like they were 'spoken', traversed by a speech that didn't transform them and couldn't translate their new uncertain situation. A protagonist of the events describes how it follows the position of leader:

> the leader is somebody who is convinced that he has always been revolutionary and communist, and he doesn't ask himself what the concrete transformation of himself and the others is [...] The leader is the one that when the assemblies don't go the way they should either because a silence takes place or because some political positions are expressed which are different from the ones of his own group, he feels that he must intervene in order to fill the verbal space or to affirm his political line against the others.[2]

In this simple and clinical diagnosis we see the groups as spaces where the attempt is made to funnel subjective transformation into revolutionary efficiency; as a result of this process the positions of the singularities that composed the groups became progressively more and more rigid and the revolutionary space, in order to remain such, imposed the most conservative patterns of behaviour within itself.

The term 'human strike' was forged to name a revolt against what is reactionary even – and above all – inside the revolt. It defines a type of strike that involves the whole of life and not only its professional side, that acknowledges exploitation in all the domains and not only at work. Even the notion of work is modified if seen from the ethical prism of human strike: activities that seem to be innocent services and loving obligations to keep the family or the couple together reveal themselves as vulgar exploitation. The human strike is a movement that could potentially contaminate anyone and that attacks the foundations of life in common; its subject isn't the proletarian or the factory worker but the whatever singularity that everyone is. This movement isn't there to reveal the exceptionality or the superiority of one group or another but to unmask the whateverness of everybody as the open secret that social classes hide.

One definition of human strike can be found in *Tiqqun 2*: it's a strike 'with no claims, that deterritorialises the agora and reveals the non-political as the place of the implicit redistribution of responsibilities and unremunerated work.'[3]

Italian feminisms offer a paradigm of this kind of action because they have claimed the abolition of the borders that made politics the territory of men. If the sexual borders of politics weren't clearly marked in the '70s in Europe, they still persisted in an obscure region of the life in common, like premonitory nightmares that never stop coming true. In 1938 Virginia Woolf wrote in *Three Guineas:*

> Inevitably we look upon societies as conspiracies that sink the private brother, whom many of us have reason to respect, and inflate in his stead a monstrous male, loud of voice, hard

of fist, childishly intent upon scoring the floor of the earth with chalk marks, within whose mystic boundaries human beings are penned, rigidly, separately, artificially; where, daubed red and gold, decorated like a savage with feathers he goes through mystic rites and enjoys the dubious pleasures of power and dominion while we, 'his' women, are locked in the private house without share in the many societies of which his society is composed.[4]

Against the chalk marks, already obsolete in 1938 but that still keep appearing beneath our steps even in the 21st century, Lia Cigarini and Luisa Muraro specified in 1992 in a text called 'Politics and Political Practice':

We don't want to separate politics from culture, love and work and we can't find any criterion for doing so. A politics of this kind, a separated one, we wouldn't like it and we wouldn't know what to do with it.[5]

At the core of this necessity of a politics that transforms life and that can be transformed by life, there wasn't a claim against injustice but the desire of finding the right voice for one's own body, in order to fight the deep feeling of being spoken by somebody else, that can be called political ventriloquism.

A quotation by Serena, published in the brochure *Sottosopra* n°3 in 1976, describes a modest miracle that took place at the women's convention in Pinarella:

after the first day and a half, something strange happened to me: there were bodies under the heads that spoke, listened, laughed; if I spoke (with what tranquil serenity and unassertiveness did I talk to two hundred women!), somehow in my words there was my body, which had found a strange way of speaking itself.[6]

What an example of miraculous transubstantiation of the human strike.

1890: Date of Birth of the Human Strike

In her extensive research around strikes in the 19th century, Michelle Perrot talks about the birth of a sort of 'sentimental strike' in the year 1890. 4 May of that year, in the newspaper from Lille entitled *Le Cri du Travailleur* (the Worker's Cry) we can read that 'the strikers didn't give any reason for their interruption of the work [...] just that they want to do the same thing as the others.' In this type of movement, young people and women start to play a very important role, Perrot says. In a small village called Vienne militant women enjoined their female comrades,

> Let's not bear this miserable conditions any longer. Let's rise up, let's claim our rights, let's fight for a more honourable place. Let's dare to say to our masters: we are just like you, made out of flesh and bones, we should live happy and free through our work.[7]

In another small village, Besseges, in the same year a young woman of 32, the wife of a miner and mother of five, Amandine Vernet, reveals her vocation of natural born leader, she never made herself noticeable before May 14th when she started to read a written speech in a meeting of 5,000 people in the Robiac woods. The day after she had started to speak, and the following days, made more self-confident by her success, she pronounced violent and moving speeches. She had the talent of making part of her audience cry.[8]

In this type of strike, what Perrot calls the emotional strike, the movement is no longer limited to a specific target: what is at stake is a transformation of subjectivity. This transformation – and that is the interesting point – is at the same time the cause and the consequence of the strike. The subjective, the social and the political changes are tightly entangled so that necessarily this type of uprising concerns subjects whose social identity is poorly codified, the people that Rancière calls the 'placeless' or the 'partless'. They are movements where people unite under the slogan 'we need to change ourselves' (Foucault), which means that the change of conditions isn't the ultimate aim but a means to change one's subjectivity and one's relationships.

According to some interpretations, there have been some components of this kind inside the movement of '68. Young people and women rose up then and claimed new rights that weren't only political in an acquired sense, but that changed the very meaning of the word 'political'.

The inclusion of sexuality as an officially political territory is actually symptomatic of this transformation. Sexuality isn't in fact the right term to employ, because it already designates an artificially separated field of reality. We should rather talk about the rehabilitation of the concept of desire, and analyse how new desires enter the political sphere in these specific moments, during the emotional strikes that we call 'human strikes'.

The feminisms that do not pursue the integration in a world conceived and shaped by male protagonists are part of these strikes. We can read about this crucial point in a collective book from 1987 entitled *Don't Believe You Have Rights* in Italian, translated as *Sexual Difference, A Theory of Social-Symbolic Practice*:

> The difference in being a woman has come into free existence not by working through the contradictions pertaining to the social body as a whole, but by working through the ones each woman experienced in herself and which did not have a social form before receiving it from female politics. In other words, it is we who have ourselves invented the social contradictions which make out freedom necessary.[9]

Here invented doesn't mean made up, but found and translated revealing their dormant political dimension.

Human Strike's Plane of Consistency

> They say it is love. We say it is unwaged work. They call it frigidity. We call it absenteeism. Every miscarriage is a work accident. Homosexuality and heterosexuality are both working conditions... but homosexuality is workers' control of production, not the end of work. More smiles? More money. Nothing will be so powerful in destroying the healing virtues

of a smile. Neuroses, suicides, desexualisation: occupational diseases of the housewife.

- Silvia Federici, 'Wages Against Housework', 1974

1. The house where we make the most part of our work (the domestic work), is atomized in thousands of places, but it's present everywhere, in town, in the countryside, on the mountains, etc.

2. We are controlled and we depend on thousands of little bosses and controllers: they are our husbands, fathers, brothers etc., but we only have one master: the State.

3. Our comrades of work and struggle, that are our neighbours, aren't physically in touch with us during the work as it happens in the factory: but we can meet in places that we know, where we all go when we can steal some free time during the day. And each one of us isn't separated from the other by qualifications and professional categories. We all make the same work.

[...] If we went on a strike we would not leave unfinished products or raw materials untransformed etc.: by interrupting our work we wouldn't paralyse the production but the daily reproduction of the working class. This would hit the heart of the Capitalist system, because it would become an actual strike even for those that normally go on strike without us; but since the moment we stop to guarantee the survival of those which we are affectively bound to, we will also have a difficulty in continuing the resistance.

- Emilia Romagna's coordination for wages for domestic work, Bologna, 1976

The worker has the possibility of joining a union, going on strike, the mothers are isolated, locked in their houses, tightened to their children by charitable bonds. Our wildcat strikes manifest themselves as a physical and mental breakdown.

– Adrienne Rich, *Of Woman Born*, 1980

The situation of not being able to draw the line between life and work, that used only to concern housewives, is now becoming generalised. A strike isn't possible to envisage for most of us, but the reasons we keep living the way we do and can't rebel against anyone but ourselves are to be searched for in our libidinal metabolism and in the libidinal economy we participate in.

Each struggle has become a struggle against a part of ourselves because we are always partly complicit with the things that oppress us. The biopower under which we live is the power that owns our bodies but allows us the right to speak.

According to what Giorgio Agamben writes in *The Coming Community*, the colonisation of physiology by industry started in the '20s and reached its peak when photography allowed a massive circulation of pornography. The anonymous bodies portrayed were absolutely whatever and because of this very reason generically desirable. Images of real human beings had become for the first time in history objects of desire on a massive scale, and therefore objects.

Stuart Ewen explains very well how advertising starts to heavily target women and young people in the '50s, right after the war; women and children were the majority of the bodies portrayed in a promiscuous proximity with consumer goods. The intimacy between things and human beings has created all sorts of symbolic disorders from the very beginning. Since then, consumption has come to shape the actual life form of human beings – not only so-called life style. In the case of women the confusion and enforced cohabitation with objects within the sphere of desire – both male and female desire – is clear for everybody. Advertisements talk to the affects, and tell tales of a human life reconciled with things, where the inexpressiveness and the hostility of objects are constantly obliterated by the joy and beauty that they are supposed to bring to their owners.

In advertising work is never really present and life has no gravity: objects have no weight, the link between the cause and the effect of gestures is governed by pure fantasy.

The dreams engendered by capitalism are the most disquieting of its products, their specific visual language is also the source of the misunderstanding between the inhabitants of the poorly developed countries and the westerners. These dreams are conceived as devices of subjectivisation, scenes from the life of the toxic community of human beings and things; where the commodity is absent, bodies are tragically different.

If taken to its conclusion this implicit philosophy leads to the complete redundancy of art – and in this sense the message that we all know so well and that we all receive every day in the streets of the cities or from the television screen must be taken seriously. The artwork is no longer the humanised object – this change started to take place in the 19th century with the industrialisation of life in general. Duchamp himself explains the birth of the readymade in 1955 in an interview with James Johnson Sweeny by declaring that he came to conceive of it as a consequence of the dehumanisation of the artwork.[10] The task of making objects expressive and responsive to human feelings, which for thousands of years had been performed by artists, is now performed by capitalism essentially through television. Because what is at stake in the capitalistic vision of the world is a continuous production of a libidinal economy in which behaviours, expressions and gestures contribute to the creation of this new human body.

Irreversable Anthropological Transformation in Italy (And Elsewhere)

I think that this generation [...] of people that were 15 or 20 years old when they made this [revolutionary] choice between 1971 and 1972, which in the following years becomes a generalised process in the factories and the schools, in the parishes, in the neighbourhoods, have gone through an anthropological transformation. I can't find a better definition, an irreversible cultural modification of themselves that you can't come back from and that's why these subjects later, after '79, when everything is over, become crazy, commit suicide, become drug addicts because of the impossibility and the intolerability of being included and tamed by the system.[11]

That's how Nanni Balestrini describes a form of tragic human strike that took place during the '80s, when the movement of '77 fell under the weight of a disproportionate repression.

The bleed of revolutionary lives from the country makes Italy a nation of the disappeared. Without needing a genocide or a real dictatorship, the strategy of tension and a modest amount of State terrorism achieved this result within a few years.

One should consider that what doesn't happen isn't a disgrace or the legitimate source of resentment against an anonymous and submissive population, but a consequence of what has happened before.

The space of politics in which Berlusconi rose to power without encountering any resistance was a territory in which any opposition had already been deported after the repression had started to function directly on life forms, and people could no longer desire in the same way because the libidinal economy they were part of had gone bankrupt.

One question that still hasn't been considered with sufficient attention in the militant context is the one of struggle-force. Struggle-force, like love-force, must be protected and regenerated. It's a resource that doesn't renovate itself automatically and needs collective conditions for its creation.

Human strike can be read as an extreme attempt to reappropriate the means of production of struggle-force, of love-force, of life-force. These means are ends in themselves; they already bring with them a new potentiality that makes subjects stronger. The political space where this operation is possible isn't of course the same one that was colonised by televisual biopower. It's the one that we can foresee in Lia's words from 1976:

> The return of the repressed threatens all my projects of work, research, politics. Does it threaten them or is it the truly political thing in myself, to which I should give relief and room? (...) The silence failed this part of myself that desired to make politics, but it affirmed something new. There has been a change, I have started to speak out, but during these days I have felt that the affirmative part of myself was occupying all the space again. I convinced myself of the fact that the mute woman is the most fertile objection to our politics. The non-political digs tunnels that we mustn't fill with earth. [12]

Columbus, 28 October 2009

Footnotes

1   Nanni Balestrini & Primo Moroni, *L'orda d'oro 1966-1977: La grande ondata rivoluzionaria e creativa, politica ed esistenziale*, Feltrinelli Editore, 1997, p.508.
2   Ibid., p.506.
3   Tiqqun, *Tiqqun 2*, Paris, 2001, p.221.
4   Virginia Wolf, *A Room of One's Own & Three Guineas*, Oxford: Oxford University Press 2008, p.308.
5   Lia Cigarini & Luisa Muraro, 'Politics and Political Practice', 1992, http://www.url.it/donnestoria/testi/percorso_900/politicaepratica.htm
6   *Sexual Difference, A Theory of Social-Symbolic Practice*, Patricia Cicogna & Teresa de Lauretis (trans.), Bloomington: Indiana University Press, 1990. *Sexual Difference* is the English translation of *Non credere di avere dei diritti*, Milan:

La Libreria delle donne di Milano, 1987.

7   Michelle Perrot, *Les ouvriers en grève*, France 1871–1890, Paris, La Haye: Mouton, 1974, p.99.

8   Ibid., pp.99–100.

9   *Sexual Difference*, op. cit.

10 See, 'Marcel Duchamp. An interview with James Johnson Sweeny, in *Wisdom: Conversations with Elder Wise Men of Our Day*, James Nelson (ed.), New York: W.W. Norton & Company, 1958, pp.89–99.

11 N. Balestrini, *L'Editore in La Grande Rivolta*, Milan: Bompiani, 1999, p.318–319.

12 *Sexual Difference*, op. cit.

EXISTENTIAL METONYMY AND IMPERCEPTIBLE ABSTRACTIONS

1. Thinking Against Ourselves

'Human strike' designates the most generic movement of revolt. The adjective 'human' in this case doesn't have any moral connotation, it is just more inclusive than 'general', because every human strike is an amoral gesture and it is never merely political or social. It attacks the economic, affective, sexual and emotional conditions that oppress people.

The interest and the difficulty of this concept lies in the fact that it is a concept that thinks against itself. And thinking against ourselves will be the necessity of the revolts to come, as desubjectivisation (taking distance from what we are, becoming something else) will be the only way to fight our exploitation. In fact our new working conditions see us being exploited as much in the workplace as outside of it, as the workplace has both exploded and liquefied and so gained our whole lives.

Thinking against ourselves will mean thinking against our identity and our effort to preserve it, it will mean stopping believing in the necessity of identifying ourselves with the place we occupy.

The movement of thought normally used to describe facts and processes of life cannot be applied to the investigation of the particular form of behaviour that we call 'human strike', because the human strike transforms the common ways of understanding and expressing things that actually entrap us in the very situations from which we must escape. Because our perception always includes the position from which we perceive.

Human strike, therefore always strikes partially against itself, and this is why when the historical toll is taken of its manifestations, as for example in the case of the feminist movements of the 1970s in Italy, it is hard to separate the constructive aspects from the destructive ones. It is difficult to bring out the positive sides, because the achievements of this kind of strike are inseparable from the lives of people, they cannot be measured in terms of numbers, wage increases or material transformations, but only in different ways of living and thinking. To the distracted gaze of a superficial spectator, a landscape crossed by human strike might even seem more damaged than radically revolutionised.

What we are looking at, then, is a movement of desubjectivisation and resubjectivisation, of exit from a condition – from a certain type of identification that goes with obligations, stereotypes and projections – and an entrance into a new state, less defined, more uncertain, but freed of the weights that burdened the previous identity and allowed the perpetuation of the status quo.

For example, when Bartleby opposes the lawyer with the inertia of his generically negative preference, he politely withdraws from the obligations of his job and revolts without directly confronting the hierarchy. His rebellion creates a ground that nothing can get a grip on, because he does not say what he would prefer to be different (he does not formulate a claim) or what he dislikes about his condition (he does not express a denunciation). His gesture robs the power of its power, at which point that the lawyer who employs him experiences inappropriate feelings for Bartleby, something akin to love, and falls prey to the impression that his virility is being shaken. The roots of his authority are undermined by the situation and he finds a part of himself, the one which takes sides with Bartleby's revolt, hostile to his own role as a boss.

2. Real Abstraction

It has happened in the past, and recently in Egypt, for example, that soldiers have deserted and joined up with the rebels during revolutions. At a certain point, a part of them begins to think and to act against themselves, urging them to abandon their position and their identity, which seemed to have been made only of obedience until the moment they flipped. But how can such a process be applied to our lives?

We need to take a step back and ask ourselves what kind of relationship exists between the knowledge, of ourselves and the world, and our subjectivity. And what is the relationship between the knowledge that others have or think they have of our subjectivity and the way this influences our potentiality.

At the risk of simplification, the Marxist tradition, through the method of historical materialism, attempted to expose the criminal abstraction of exchange relationships within capitalist societies. It shed light on the real relationships, stripped of the features of social classes, based on rapacious disparities which contradict the physiological equality of human beings.

According to Alfred Sohn-Rethel, the two famous initial chapters of Marx's *Capital*, in which the mysterious nature of commodities is described and explained, should be re-examined in the light of a problem. For Marx, commodity is the only abstraction that is not a product of thought but of behaviour, namely that of exchange or 'exchangism', as he calls it:

> If in *Capital* the fundamental epistemological meaning of the Marxian discovery of real abstraction does not become explicit, this is due to the fact that this discovery has to do with the domain of political economy and not that of knowledge.[1]

In other words, the separation between theory and practice, that makes thought myopic and unsuited to understanding its unconscious relationship with the commodity, causes the impossibility of formulating this state of things (abstraction being realised through shared habits) as a problem located between thought and life, one that must be confronted by any revolt. Elsewhere, Sohn-Rethel even writes that:

> the expression 'historical materialist theory of knowledge' is a contradiction in terms. The concept of 'knowledge', as it is understood by all theoretical philosophy and all theory of knowledge from its beginnings (with Pythagoras, Heraclitus and Parmenides), all the way to Wittgenstein and Bertrand Russell, etc., is a fetishistic concept that creates an ideal figure of 'knowledge in general', a knowledge deprived of any link to the historical and economic context.[2]

A suspected proximity in fact exists between the birth of Greek philosophy, with its categories abstracted from social relations and derived from nature, and the creation of the first currencies that begin to circulate precisely at the same time as concepts like the substance or the Parmenidean One. According to Sohn-Rethel, a true *perceptive incompatibility* exists between the tool used (the theory of knowledge we have inherited, which comes from a secret complicity with capitalism) and the object that we are trying to visualise (social and human relations within society).

Basically, the types of knowledge applied to the processes of subjectivisation and revolt are pernicious variations of idealism that conserve the division between hand and head – which is, in his view, the root of the impossibility of communism. This separation between head and hand, of course, corresponds to the division between intellectual and material labour, but also to the inevitable schizophrenia between our working self and our affective self, between our analytical self and our practical self, our political self and our existential self. There is a gap between the being that we are within oppressive relationships, in everyday relationships in general, and the being who is capable of analysing them and putting them at a distance, of describing the causes of the political impotence that afflicts us. And in this gap the pertinence of the analyses is worthless, and cannot allow us to transform our lives. The same subject, in short, cannot see himself in a given situation and find a theoretical way to get practically out of it, because he thinks from the position in which he finds himself, with what is available to him in that condition. If other tools were available to him, immediately his condition would be a different one.

3. Existential Metonymy

But let's examine the problem from another perspective. Starting from the moment in which this particular commodity – currency – is created, whose function is to be a means of exchange about which we can say that its use value is only that of permitting exchange value. We can also say that there are equivalent behaviours in our society, uses of the self whose function is identical to that of currency. We could even formulate the hypothesis that as the value-form contaminates the entire realm of objects, including those that are not commodities, in the same way the value-form that injects exchange value into behaviours colonises or infects all human behaviours (including the most spontaneous, emotional and disinterested).

These social relations are imperceptible abstractions as such – exactly like the exchange abstraction, about which Sohn-Rethel writes that 'being conscious of the abstraction as it is taking place is an impossibility in itself, because the abstraction would not be produced if the consciousness was focused on the abstraction instead of the exchange.'[3] This abstraction-distraction, in fact, prevents us from applying to our behaviour, in order to transform it, the very thought that made that behaviour possible. If we believe in exchange value and enter into the behaviour of exchange – in which we are already constantly immersed – we cannot understand, at the same time, the way in which this behaviour constitutes an absurdity. The paradox is that commercial exchange truly is a social link created by an activity that denies it, because the use of currency allows every owner of commodities to abstractedly (but concretely) pursue his own personal interest, without obstacles, without ever thinking about society.[4] Sohn-Rethel describes this phenomenon as 'practical solipsism':

> the formal identity of the 'private' self [of the owners of commodities] is abstracted from their existence and the interests of that existence, and has no other reality than that of pure thought. This principle, although it isn't consciously understood, is certainly part of the exchange abstraction [...] It is the subject of the apperception, which apperceives the exchange abstraction and its various elements.[5]

Apperception is the perception we have of the fact of perceiving. Aristotle writes in *De Anima* something extraordinary about this faculty when applied to sight:

> if to perceive by sight is just to see, and what is seen is colour (and the thing that has colour), then if we are to see that which sees, that which sees originally must be coloured. It is clear therefore that 'to perceive by sight' has more than one meaning; for even when we are not seeing, it is by sight that we discriminate darkness from light. So the principle of sight itself somehow has a colour.[6]

Centuries after Aristotle, Marcel Broodthaers wrote, in *The Crow and the Fox (After La Fontaine)*, in which he revisited the famous fable by La Fontaine:

> The crow and the fox are absent. I can hardly remember them. I have forgotten the paws and hands, the games and costumes, the voices and colours, the shrewdness and vanity. The painter was all colours. The architect was made

out of stone. The crow and the fox were made of printed characters.[7]

The qualities sensorially perceived, the properties of these beings or of the coloured objects, are so deeply associated with our senses that they must somehow be made of a similar fabric in order to be perceptible, just as the architect must partly be made of stone in order to be able to build. This metonymic materialism, which returns in Broodthaers's poem as in a dream and gives rise to the observations of Aristotle on coloured vision as a scientific intuition, can perhaps more clearly shed light on the question of the perception of the possible, on how subjects can come to know their own potentiality.

Agamben comments on this same passage from *De Anima* in 'On Potentiality', writing that when Aristotle asks 'why is it that in the absence of external objects the senses do not give any sensation?' the answer is: because in that case the sensation is a potentiality, but not yet realised.[8] The physical organ related to the colour or to the material literally sleeps in their absence, at a point that we might not even know that we can perceive something if the occasion for doing so never presented itself; then our coloured self, our stone-like self, remains mysterious and hidden and we'll never be painters or architects.

Freedom *is* a perceptible fabric within society and it is a part of subjectivity that can be activated – as revolutions and insurrections historically prove – but it cannot be known without being experienced.

Our apperception itself must be stimulated in order to get thought out of its natural state of astonishment and to free it from what Deleuze calls 'the philosophical good will'. A different, poetic form of materialism is needed in order to short-circuit this state of things, to bring daylight into this dark zone of legibility of the past and present that is our potentiality.

4. Witnessing by Means of Life

The human strike as a social practice brings with it a form of theoretical-practical knowledge that immediately troubles the hierarchies of the society of exchange, because it is supposed to make economic relations emerge where we only see social, or even just human relations.

There is a form of existential metonymy that consists in transforming the self into a tool for the creation of visibility. Foucault has called this type of practice 'witnessing by means of life'. In a lecture given on 29 February 1984, shortly prior to his death, Foucault focused on the 'life-form as the living scandal of truth', and 'of the lifestyle and life-form as the place where truth emerges.'[9] The ethical problem of living according to one's convictions is not exactly what is addressed in this research. What Foucault was trying to grasp, even in their most eruptive and explosive forms (such as Russian nihilism, anarchism and terrorism in general), as 'practices of life until death for truth', is the way in which subjects have managed to transform a theoretical and political viewpoint into a practice of life, though perhaps one that is wild or extreme. Revolution within the modern European world, he writes, hasn't only been a political project but also a life-form. If one analyses the ways in which life as a revolutionary activity or the revolutionary activity as a life have been organised and regulated, accordingly to Foucault, one can find three forms: the secret sociability (secret societies and clandestine resistance groups); the instituted organisation (the political parties and official organisations), and the witness through life which is a kind of militancy taking the form of a style of existence. This style must rupture the conventions, the habits and the values of society, 'it must manifest directly, by its visible form, its constant practice, and its immediate existence, the concrete possibility and the evident value of an *other* life, which is the true life.'[10] Making life into a weapon and a battleground at the same time is the specificity of this third aspect of revolutionary life. In this specific case lifestyle is supposed to act as the incarnation of truth and the display of a certain set of values, but it is also a concrete and direct contestation of other people's ways of life. Cynicism in its original form – which is the starting point of this course by Foucault – was a philosophy that went with a certain ethics made from poverty, scandal and nudity that were all ways of manifesting the truth against social conventions and conformist habits. Where human strike touches these matters is in the fact that adopting a different behaviour materially deregulates the social machine and causes the appearance of the disturbing truth of freedom and an image of a possible life. The capitalist system for example does carry an image, or several images, of life that, if not embodied by people, cause it to fail.

5. Barbarous Truth and Imageless Politics

Human strike certainly is a way of witnessing by means of life, but it is never an exemplary gesture. Its logics are simply different from and incompatible with those that lie behind the submission of our subjectivity to the world as it is, and first of all they are incompatible with the logic of commodities, which is supposed to be the load-bearing wall of the architecture of our interests.

When we talk about existential metonymy we are talking about a new materialism that takes the need for freedom as a truer reality than market speculations or the fluctuations of currency exchange rates. Our potentiality can only become perceptible for us if we free ourselves of the parasite of the economy and refuse to think only the thinkable.

Curiously enough, Foucault concluded the course of 29 February 1984 by talking about art as a form of scandalous rupture. In the modern world, he writes,

> art itself, be it literature, painting or music, has to establish a relationship with the real that is no longer a matter of ornament, of imitation, but a matter or laying bare, unmasking, scraping, digging, of violent reduction to the basic aspects of existence. [...] Art becomes a place of eruption from below, of what has no right or possibility of expression in a culture. [...] The courage of art in its barbarous truth should go against the consensus of the culture.

This quote that almost seems reminiscent of Benjamin's concept of positive barbarism opens up a different space of abstraction that appears related to the abandonment of representation as a political and existential practice. What happens in modern and contemporary art seems here to carry the formula for a possibility that could be transposed in other territories of reality. If representation is the reproduction of a model (in a figurative sense as much as in a political one) then this radical refusal for imitation could lead, if extended, to an imageless politics, something that doesn't need to reproduce any existing experience or structure, a politics of potentiality based on the materiality of this barbarous truth.

Vancouver, 15 October 2012

Footnotes

1   Alfred Sohn-Rethel, 'Travail intellectuel et travail manuel' in *La pensée marchadise*, Editions du Croquant, Broissieux, 2010, p.119.

2   Ibid., p.74.

3   Ibid., p.94.

4   Ibid., p.140.

5   Ibid., p.139.

6   Aristotle, Chapter 2, Book III, *De Anima (On the Soul)*, Penguin Classics, 1987.

7   Marcel Broodthaers, *Le Corbeau et le Renard (d'après La Fontaine)* (1967) film, 16mm, colour, 7'.

8   Giorigio Agamben, 'On Potentiality', in *Potentialities: Collected Essays in Philosophy*, Standford: Stanford University Press, 199, p.178.

9   Michel Foucault, 'Ten: 29 February 1984, Second Hour', *The Courage of Truth: The Government of the Self and Others II, Lectures at the Collège de France*, 1983-4, Graham Burchell (trans.), Basingstoke: Palgrave Macmillan, 2011, pp.177-190.

10 Ibid., p.184.

Printed in April 2021
by Rotomail Italia S.p.A., Vignate (MI) - Italy